Practical Machine Learning
Innovations in Recommendation

Ted Dunning and Ellen Friedman

Beijing · Cambridge · Farnham · Köln · Sebastopol · Tokyo

Practical Machine Learning

by Ted Dunning and Ellen Friedman

Printed in the United States of America.

Published by O'Reilly Media, Inc., 1005 Gravenstein Highway North, Sebastopol, CA 95472.

O'Reilly books may be purchased for educational, business, or sales promotional use. Online editions are also available for most titles (*http://my.safaribooksonline.com*). For more information, contact our corporate/institutional sales department: 800-998-9938 or *corporate@oreilly.com*.

Editor: Mike Loukides

January 2014: First Edition

Revision History for the First Edition:

2014-01-22: First release

2014-08-15: Second release

See *http://oreilly.com/catalog/errata.csp?isbn=9781491915387* for release details.

ISBN: 978-1-491-91538-7

[LSI]

Table of Contents

CHAPTER 1

Practical Machine Learning

A key to one of most sophisticated and effective approaches in machine learning and recommendation is contained in the observation: "I want a pony." As it turns out, building a simple but powerful recommender is much easier than most people think, and wanting a pony is part of the key.

Machine learning, especially at the scale of huge datasets, can be a daunting task. There is a dizzying array of algorithms from which to choose, and just making the choice between them presupposes that you have sufficiently advanced mathematical background to understand the alternatives and make a rational choice. The options are also changing, evolving constantly as a result of the work of some very bright, very dedicated researchers who are continually refining existing algorithms and coming up with new ones.

What's a Person To Do?

The good news is that there's a new trend in machine learning and particularly in recommendation: very simple approaches are proving to be very effective in real-world settings. Machine learning is moving from the research arena into the pragmatic world of business. In that world, time to reflect is very expensive, and companies generally can't afford to have systems that require armies of PhDs to run them. Practical machine learning weighs the trade-offs between the most advanced and accurate modeling techniques and the costs in real-world terms: what approaches give the best results in a cost-benefit sense?

Let's focus just on recommendation. As you look around, it's obvious that some very large companies have for some years put machine learning into use at large scale (see Figure 1-1).

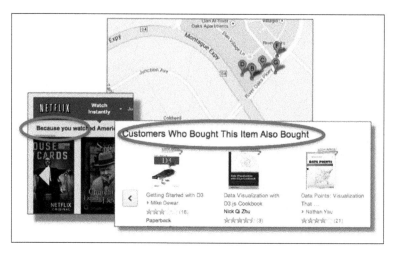

Figure 1-1. What does recommendation look like?

As you order items from Amazon, a section lower on the screen suggests other items that might be of interest, whether it be O'Reilly books, toys, or collectible ceramics. The items suggested for you are based on items you've viewed or purchased previously. Similarly, your video-viewing choices on Netflix influence the videos suggested to you for future viewing. Even Google Maps adjusts what you see depending on what you request; for example, if you search for a tech company in a map of Silicon Valley, you'll see that company and other tech companies in the area. If you search in that same area for the location of a restaurant, other restaurants are now marked in the area. (And maybe searching for a big data meetup should give you technology companies plus pizza places.)

But what does machine learning recommendation look like under the covers? Figure 1-2 shows the basics.

$$\begin{bmatrix} A_1 & A_2 \end{bmatrix}' \begin{bmatrix} A_1 & A_2 \end{bmatrix} = \begin{bmatrix} A_1' \\ A_2' \end{bmatrix} \begin{bmatrix} A_1 & A_2 \end{bmatrix}$$

$$= \begin{bmatrix} A_1'A_1 & A_1'A_2 \\ A_2'A_1 & A_2'A_2 \end{bmatrix}$$

$$\begin{bmatrix} r_1 \\ r_2 \end{bmatrix} = \begin{bmatrix} A_1'A_1 & A_1'A_2 \\ A_2'A_1 & A_2'A_2 \end{bmatrix} \begin{bmatrix} h_1 \\ h_2 \end{bmatrix}$$

$$r_1 = A_1'A_1h_1 + A_1'A_2h_2$$

Figure 1-2. The math may be scary, but if approached in the right way, the concepts underlying how to build a recommender are easily understood.

If you love matrix algebra, this figure is probably a form of comfort food. If not, you may be among the majority of people looking for solutions to machine-learning problems who want something more approachable. As it turns out, there are some innovations in recommendation that make it much easier and more powerful for people at all levels of expertise.

There are a few ways to deal with the challenge of designing recommendation engines. One is to have your own team of engineers and data scientists, all highly trained in machine learning, to custom design recommenders to meet your needs. Big companies such as Google, Twitter, and Yahoo! are able to take that approach, with some very valuable results.

Other companies, typically smaller ones or startups, hope for success with products that offer drag-and-drop approaches that simply require them to supply a data source, click on an algorithm, and look for easily understandable results to pop out via nice visualization tools. There are lots of new companies trying to design such semiautomated products, and given the widespread desire for a turnkey solution, many of these new products are likely to be financially successful. But designing really effective recommendation systems requires some careful thinking, especially about the choice of data and how it is handled. This is true even if you have a fairly automated way of selecting and applying an algorithm. Getting a recommendation model to run is one thing; getting it to provide effective recommendations is quite a lot of work. Surprisingly to some, the fancy math and algorithms are only a small part of that effort. Most of the effort required to build a good recommendation system is put into getting the right data to the recommendation engine in the first place.

If you can afford it, a different way to get a recommendation system is to use the services of a high-end machine-learning consultancy. Some of these companies have the technical expertise necessary to supply stunningly fast and effective models, including recommenders. One way they achieve these results is by throwing a huge collection of algorithms at each problem, and—based on extensive experience in analyzing such situations—selecting the algorithm that gives the best outcome. SkyTree is an example of this type of company, with its growing track record of effective machine learning models built to order for each customer.

Making Recommendation Approachable

A final approach is to do it yourself, even if you or your company lack access to a team of data scientists. In the past, this hands-on approach would have been a poor option for small teams. Now, with new developments in algorithms and architecture, small-scale development teams can build large-scale projects. As machine learning becomes more practical and approachable, and with some of the innovations and suggestions in this paper, the self-built recommendation engine becomes much easier and effective than you may think.

Why is this happening? Resources for Apache Hadoop–based computing are evolving and rapidly spreading, making projects with very large-scale datasets much more approachable and affordable. And the ability to collect and save more data from web logs, sensor data, social media, etc., means that the size and number of large datasets is also growing.

How is this happening? Making recommendation practical depends in part on making it simple. But not just any simplification will do, as explained in Chapter 2.

Careful Simplification

Make things as simple as possible, but not simpler.

— Roger Sessions
Simplifying Einstein's quote

"Keep it simple" is becoming the mantra for successful work in the big data sphere, especially for Hadoop-based computing. Every step saved in an architectural design not only saves time (and therefore money), but it also prevents problems down the road. Extra steps leave more chances for operational errors to be introduced. In production, having fewer steps makes it easier to focus effort on steps that are essential, which helps keep big projects operating smoothly. Clean, streamlined architectural design, therefore, is a useful goal.

But choosing the right way to simplify isn't all that simple—you need to be able to recognize when and how to simplify for best effect. A major skill in doing so is to be able to answer the question, "How good is good?" In other words, sometimes there is a trade-off between simple designs that produce effective results and designs with additional layers of complexity that may be more accurate on the same data. The added complexity may give a slight improvement, but in the end, is this improvement worth the extra cost? A nominally more accurate but considerably more complex system may fail so often that the net result is lower overall performance. A complex system may also be so difficult to implement that it distracts from other tasks with a higher payoff, and that is very expensive.

This is not to say that complexity is never advantageous. There certainly are systems where the simple solution is not good enough and where complexity pays off. Google's search engine is one such example;

machine translation is another. In the case of recommendation, there are academic approaches that produce infinitesimally better results than simpler approaches but that literally require hundreds of complex mathematical models to cooperate to produce recommendations. Such systems are vastly more complex than the simple recommender described in this paper. In contrast, there are minor extensions of the simple recommender described here, such as multimodal recommendations, that can have dramatically positive effects on accuracy. The point is, look for the simplest solution that gives you results that are good enough for your goals and target your efforts. Simplify, but simplify smart.

How do you do that? In machine learning, knowing which algorithms really matter is a huge advantage. Recognizing similarities in use cases that on the surface appear very different but that have underlying commonalities can let you reuse simple, robust architectural design patterns that have already been tested and that have a good track record.

Behavior, Co-occurrence, and Text Retrieval

Smart simplification in the case of recommendation is the focus of this paper. This simplification includes an outstanding innovation that makes it *much* easier to build a powerful recommender than most people expect. The recommender relies on the following observations:

1. Behavior of users is the best clue to what they want.

2. Co-occurrence is a simple basis that allows Apache Mahout to compute significant indicators of what should be recommended.

3. There are similarities between the weighting of indicator scores in output of such a model and the mathematics that underlie text-retrieval engines.

4. This mathematical similarity makes it possible to exploit text-based search to deploy a Mahout recommender using Apache Solr/Lucene.

Design of a Simple Recommender

The simple recommender uses a two-part design to make computation efficient and recommendation fast. Co-occurrence analysis and extraction of indicators is done offline, ahead of time. The algorithms used in this analysis are described in Chapter 4. The online part of the recommender uses recent actions by the target user to query an Apache Solr search engine and is able to return recommendations quickly.

Let's see how this works.

CHAPTER 3

What I Do, Not What I Say

One of the most important steps in any machine-learning project is data extraction. Which data should you choose? How should it be prepared to be appropriate input for your machine-learning model?

In the case of recommendation, the choice of data depends in part on what you think will best reveal what users want to do—what they like and do not like—such that the recommendations your system offers are effective. The best choice of data may surprise you—it's not user ratings. What a user actually does usually tells you much more about her preferences than what she claims to like when filling out a customer ratings form. One reason is that the ratings come from a subset of your user pool (and a skewed one at that—it's comprised of the users who like [or at least are willing] to rate content). In addition, people who feel strongly in the positive or negative about an item or option may be more motivated to rate it than those who are somewhat neutral, again skewing results. We've seen some cases where no more than a few percent of users would rate content.

Furthermore, most people do not entirely understand their own likes and dislikes, especially where new and unexplored activities are concerned. The good news is that there is a simple solution: you can watch what a user does instead of just what he says in ratings. Of course it is not enough to watch one or a few users; those few observations will not give you a reliable way to make recommendations. But if you look at what everybody in a crowd does, you begin to get useful clues on which to base your recommender.

Behavior of a crowd helps us understand what individuals will do.

Collecting Input Data

Relying on user behavior as the input data for your recommender is a simple idea, but you have to be clever in the ways you look for data that adequately describes the behaviors that will give you useful clues for recommendation, and you have capture and process that data. You can't analyze what you don't collect.

There are many different options, but let's take a look at a widespread one: behavior of visitors on a website. Try this exercise: pick a popular website that makes use of recommendation, such as Amazon. Go there, browse the site, and have a friend observe your behavior. What do you click on or hover over? When do you scroll down? And if you were a serious visitor to the site, what might you buy?

All these behaviors provide clues about your interests, tastes, and priorities. The next question is whether or not the website analytics are capturing them in logs. Also consider any behaviors that might have been useful but were missed because of the design of the user interface for the site. What changes or additions to the page might have encouraged a useful action that could be recorded in web logs?

More and more, websites are being designed so that much or even nearly all interaction by the users is with software that runs in the browser itself. The servers for the website will occasionally be asked for a batch of data, but it is only in the context of the browser itself that the user's actions can be seen. In such browser-centric systems, it's important to record significant actions that users take and get that record back to servers for recommendation analysis. Often, the part of recommendation-system implementation that takes the most calendar time is simply adding sufficient logging to the user interface itself. Given that lag and the fact that you probably want to analyze months' worth of data, it sometimes makes sense to start recording behavioral data a good long while before starting to implement your recommendation system.

Once you have the data you need, what kind of analysis will you be doing? This is where the ponies come in.

CHAPTER 4

Co-occurrence and Recommendation

Once you've captured user histories as part of the input data, you're ready to build the recommendation model using co-occurrence. So the next question is: how does co-occurrence work in recommendations? Let's take a look at the theory behind the machine-learning model that uses co-occurrence (but without the scary math).

Think about three people: Alice, Charles, and Bob. We've got some user-history data about what they want (inferentially, anyway) based on what they bought (see Figure 4-1).

Figure 4-1. User behavior is the clue to what you should recommend.

In this toy microexample, we would predict that Bob would like a puppy. Alice likes apples and puppies, and because we know Bob likes apples, we will predict that he wants a puppy, too. Hence our starting this paper by suggesting that observations as simple as "I want a pony" are key to making a recommendation model work. Of course, real recommendations depend on user-behavior histories for huge numbers of users, not this tiny sample—but our toy example should give you an idea of how a recommender model works.

So, back to Bob. As it turns out, Bob did want a puppy, but he also wants a pony. So do Alice, Charles, and a new user in the crowd, Amelia. They *all* want a pony (we do, too). Where does that leave us?

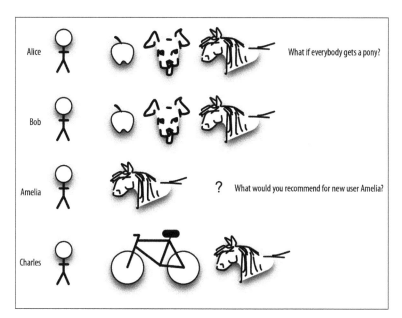

Figure 4-2. A widely popular item isn't much help as an indicator of what to recommend because it is the same for almost everybody.

The problem is, if everybody gets a pony, it's not a very good indicator of what else to predict (see Figure 4-2). It's too common of a behavior, like knowing that almost everybody buys toilet tissue or clicks on the home page on a website.

What we are looking for in user histories is not only co-occurrence of items that is interesting or *anomalous* co-occurrence. And with millions or even hundreds of millions of users and items, it's too much for a human to understand in detail. That's why we need machine learning to make that decision for us so that we can provide good recommendations.

How Apache Mahout Builds a Model

For our practical recommender, we are going to use an algorithm from the open source, scalable machine-learning library Apache Mahout to construct the recommendation model. What we want is to use Mahout's matrix algebra to get us from user-behavior histories to useful indicators for recommendation. We will build three matrices for that purpose:

History matrix
> Records the interactions between users and items as a user-by-item matrix

Co-occurrence matrix
> Transforms the history matrix into an item-by-item matrix, recording which items appeared together in user histories

Indicator matrix
> Retains only the anomalous (interesting) co-occurrences that will be the clues for recommendation

Figure 4-3 shows how we would represent that with our toy example.

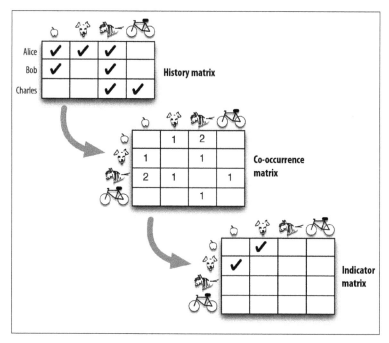

Figure 4-3. User history → co-occurrence → indicator matrix. Our model, represented by the indicator matrix, encodes the fact that apple is an indicator for recommending "puppy."

Mahout's `ItemSimilarityJob` runs the `RowSimilarityJob`, which in turn uses the log likelihood ratio test (LLR) to determine which co-occurrences are sufficiently anomalous to be of interest as indicators. So our "everybody wants a pony" observation is correct but not one of the indicators for recommendation.

Relevance Score

In order to make recommendations, we want to use items in recent user history as a query to find all items in our collection that have those recent history items as indicators. But we also want to have some way to sort items offered as recommendations in order of relevance. To do this, indicator items can be given a relevance score that is the sum of weights for each indicator. You can think of this step as giving bonus points to indicators that are most likely to give a good recommendation because they indicate something unusual or interesting about a person's interests.

Ubiquitous items (such as ponies) are not even considered to be indicators. Fairly common indicators should have small weights. Rare indicators should have large weights. Relevance for each item to be recommended depends on the size of the sum of weighted values for indicators. Items with a large relevance score will be recommended first.

At this point, we have, in theory, all that we need to produce useful recommendations, but not yet in a manner to be used in practice. How do we deliver the recommendations to users? What will trigger the recommendations, and how do we do this in a timely manner?

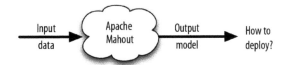

In the practical recommender design, we exploit search-engine technology to easily deploy the recommender for production. Text retrieval, also known as text search, lets us store and update indicators and metadata for items, and it provides a way to quickly find items with the best indicator scores to be offered in recommendation in real time. As a bonus, a search engine lets us do conventional search as well. Among possible search engines that we could use, we chose to use Apache Solr to deploy our recommendation model. The benefits are enormous, as described in Chapter 5.

Deploy the Recommender

Before we discuss in more detail why search technology such as Solr or Elasticsearch is a good and practical choice to deploy a recommendation engine in production, let's take a quick look at what Apache Solr and Apache Lucene actually are.

What Is Apache Solr/Lucene?

The Apache Lucene project produces two primary software artifacts. One is called Lucene-Core (usually abbreviated to simply Lucene) and the other is called Solr. Lucene-Core is a software library that provides functions to support a document-oriented sort of database that is particularly good at text retrieval. Solr is a web application that provides a full, working web service to simplify access to the capabilities of Lucene-Core. For convenience in this discussion, we will mostly just say "Solr" since it is not necessary to access the Lucene-Core library directly for recommendations.

Data loaded into a Solr index is put into *collections*. Each collection is made up of *documents*. The document contains specific information about the item in *fields*. If the fields are *indexed*, then they become searchable by Solr's retrieval capabilities. It is this search capability that we exploit to deploy the recommender. If fields are *stored*, they can be displayed to users in a web interface.

Why Use Apache Solr/Lucene to Deploy?

Lucene, which is at the heart of Solr, works by taking words (usually called "terms") in the query and attaching a weight to each one. Then Solr examines every document that contains any of the query terms and accumulates a score for each document according to the weights of the terms that document contains. Rare terms are given large weights, and common ones get small weights. Documents that accumulate high scores are taken to be more relevant than documents that do not, therefore the search results are ordered by descending score.

Remarkably, the way that Solr scores documents based on the presence of query terms in the document is very nearly the same mathematically as the desired scoring for recommendations based on the presence of indicators. This mathematical coincidence makes Solr a very attractive vehicle for deploying indicator-based recommendations.

Furthermore, Solr is deployed widely in all kinds of places. As such, it has enormous accumulated runtime and corresponding maturity. That track record makes it very attractive for building stable systems.

What's the Connection Between Solr and Co-occurrence Indicators?

Back to Bob, apples, and puppies. We need a title, description, and other metadata about all the items in order to recommend them. We store the metadata for each item in Solr in fields in a conventional way with one document per item. Figure 5-1 shows how a document for "puppy" might look in a Solr index.

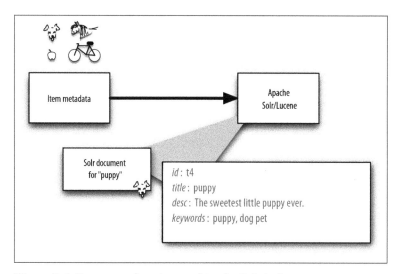

Figure 5-1. Item metadata is stored in the Solr index.

The final step of offline learning is to use Solr to deploy the recommendation model by populating a new field in each Solr item document with the indicator IDs discovered for that item. This indicator field is added to the Solr document you've already created. The result of the deployment is shown in Figure 5-2, where an "indicators" field has been added to the puppy document and contains the single indicator: apple.

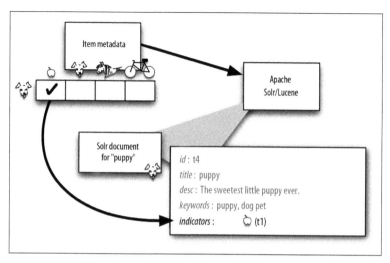

Figure 5-2. Indicator IDs making up the Mahout model are stored in the new field of the same document in Solr index.

This toy example illustrates how user-behavior data and Mahout can be used to find indicators for recommendation, and how these indicators can be stored in Solr documents for each item. Now you are ready for a detailed description of how real recommenders are implemented based on this design.

How the Recommender Works

In order to build a recommender using a search engine, we have to connect the input in the form of logs to a program from the Apache Mahout library to do the co-occurrence analysis, and from there to a search engine that actually delivers the recommendations to our users.

In an academic sense, analyzing historical user/item interactions to create indicators and deploying these indicators to a search engine is all we really need to do to create a recommendation engine. Practically speaking, however, to create a real-world recommendation engine that actually does useful work, there are a number of practical issues that have to be addressed:

- We have to present enough information on the items being recommended so that users can make sense of the recommendations. This means that we have to load additional data known as item metadata into the search engine so that the recommendation results are intelligible.

- We have to convert files into alternative forms in a number of places.
- We have to make provisions for updating recommendations and item metadata in a live system.
- We have to provide a way to integrate the recommendation results into a live and usually preexisting system.
- We have to provide a way to do testing of alternative settings and data sources.
- We have to provide ways for the operators of the system to understand whether it is working correctly or not.

You may have noticed that almost all of these issues are exactly the same as the issues involved in creating a working search engine and have therefore been nicely addressed in Solr. In particular, Solr allows documents to have fields that segregate different kinds of data and allow them to be handled differently during searches or at presentation time. Solr also provides extensive diagnostics; produces logs of searches, results, and timings; and allows ad hoc queries to be done at any time. As a result, pretty much all we have to do is add the plumbing to convert and move data through the system between components in order to get a basic recommendation engine running. Beyond that, all we have to do is elaborate the data stored in the database and the queries used to search that data to get even more advanced capabilities.

Two-Part Design

The design we are describing is for an item-based recommender that has two parts: one offline and one online. Another benefit of our design for simplifying a recommendation engine by combining Mahout and Solr is that the time-intensive parts of the work can be done ahead of time in an offline fashion.

The two parts of the design are:

Offline learning
  Load Solr with metadata for items and precompute indicators with Mahout-derived model

Online recommendation

Rapid response by Solr search to offer realtime recommendations that are triggered by recent event user histories

The *offline* steps of the two-part design are shown in Figure 5-3.

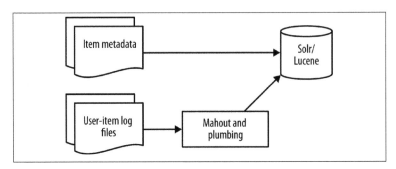

Figure 5-3. Offline learning: Basic item metadata is loaded into Solr. Mahout independently generates indicators that are updated each time the log analysis is run.

In this figure, the top path represents basic item metadata being stored in Solr. To accomplish that, item metadata is converted to Solr's native JSON format and uploaded directly to Solr using the native REST interface that Solr provides. This typically is done once to load all of the item metadata and then again as updates are received.

User-history log files are used as input for Mahout in order to derive the contents of the indicator fields through co-occurrence, very much like we did with our puppies and ponies. These indicators are reformatted and uploaded for Solr to index. This is represented by the lower path in the figure.

The co-occurrence analysis that generates indicators is typically done every night. In this analysis, user-item interactions are read from log files. These logs are transformed to discard extraneous data and to convert data formats as required by the Mahout ItemSimilarityJob. The result of the ItemSimilarityJob is then converted to Solr's native JSON format and uploaded as field-level updates to Solr.

Once the indicators are uploaded to Solr by the offline analysis, the system is ready to make recommendations in real time. Typically, before a new set of indicators goes live, ad hoc searches are performed at the Solr level to spot check the quality of the metadata and indicators and to verify that the appropriate queries produce sensible recommendations.

Realtime recommendations are generated as shown in Figure 5-4.

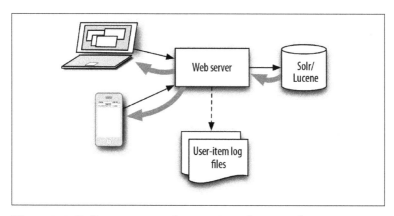

Figure 5-4. Online recommendations: In order to produce recommendations in real time, the browser on a user's computer or mobile device sends a query to the web server. This query is composed from the recent events for the user in question. The web server augments this query as necessary with additional requirements and sends the query to Solr, which responds (larger arrows) with recommendation results. The web server then returns those results to the browser. Meanwhile, user actions are stored in user logs for later processing to generate new indicators.

In this figure, users connect to a web server from any kind of device they might have. This web server records the activity of the users in logs and passes portions of that history to Solr in the form of a query on the indicator fields for items. Solr returns raw result lists, and the web server formats these results for presentation to the user. The logs produced by this server and others are exactly the logs that are given back to the overnight co-occurrence analysis that finds the indicators used in the searches.

Note that the form of the queries that are presented to Solr by the web server doesn't need to stay constant. The form of the query and even which fields are searched can be changed, and that can result in changes to how the recommendation engine works. If the web server uses templates to generate these queries, it is possible to emulate many different recommendation engines with a single Solr instance (which is large) and many templates (which are tiny). This capability can be used to do testing on alternative recommendation strategies.

Similarly, the results passed back to the user from Solr need not be passed through without any changes. Business logic can be implemented in the web server that adjusts which items are shown and in what order. This can be used to avoid recommending out-of-stock items or to adjust the diversity of the results.

The search capacities of Solr are what make realtime recommendations possible. Users implicitly provide new event histories by accessing the web server for our user interface via a variety of devices. These short-term histories are collected either in server profiles on the server or in the user's browser, then formed into queries that use the indicator fields in the Solr collection. Items retrieved by Solr based on these queries are offered as recommendations. User actions are also logged and later used to fuel the next offline analysis.

Up to this point, we have described end-to-end the simple but powerful two-part design for a recommender that has offline learning and online recommendation. This description started with the observation of behavior of many users and went through use of a machine-learning model deployed using search technology. Now let's take a look at an actual recommender that was built according to this plan.

CHAPTER 6

Example: Music Recommender

One of the best ways to learn how a recommender works is to put your hands on one. With that in mind, we developed a concrete example of a recommender for a machine-learning course developed by MapR Technologies, a distributed computing platform company, with help from a training and consulting company, Big Data Partnership. The recommender is for a mock business, Music Machine. We explore it here to illustrate what we've covered so far.

Business Goal of the Music Machine

This mock music company wants to increase stickiness for their web-based music-listening site by offering visitors enticing music recommendations that will keep them on the site longer and keep them coming back.

The business is a figment of the authors' imagination, but the music-recommendation engine and non-public Music Machine website (see Figure 6-1) are real. They provide a working example of a simple in-production recommender built according to the design we've been discussing.

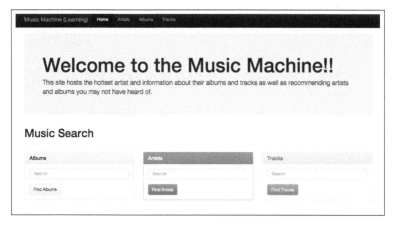

Figure 6-1. Screenshot of the mock music-listening website for which a real Mahout-Solr recommender was built.

Online businesses with similar goals are quite real and widespread, and you have most likely encountered them yourself, whether the items of interest were music, books, new cars, destinations, or something else.

Data Sources

Two types of data are needed for the music recommender: metadata about the items (artists, albums, tracks) for music that will be recommended and histories of the behavior of a large number of site visitors to serve as the training data for the Apache Mahout analysis system. Where did we get such data for our imaginary company?

The music (item) data came from the Music Brainz database, which is a public-domain database of music information. The Music Brainz database was downloaded directly from the MusicBrainz website (*http://musicbrainz.org/*) and imported into a Postgres database. The tables that describe artists and records were simplified and dumped directly from Postgres in tab-delimited format that could be imported directly into Apache Solr. As described earlier, the uploading was done as one large task when the recommender was being built. Updates to the database can be imported into Solr as new music is made available.

The logs containing user behavior historical data were generated using random-number generators that simulated listeners who did a random walk among musical genres. This is a very simple model that allows some plausible recommendations to be made, but it does not fully emulate real users. These simulated listening logs were formatted as CSV data to emulate data as a web server might collect it. The quality of the recommendations in the demonstration system are primarily limited by the quality of the synthetic data. Much as with a real system, getting more and better data would make a large difference in quality of the recommendations.

Figure 6-2 shows a small excerpt from one of these synthetic logs. In this log, we see events that start 9,669 seconds (simulated time) from the beginning of the simulation in which user 119 listens first to a song from artist 683689 (Benny Goodman) and then to a song from artist 2461 (Duke Ellington).

```
9669,BEACON,119,683689,10627847
9679,BEACON,119,683689,10627847
9689,BEACON,119,683689,10627847
9694,FINISH,119,683689,10627847
9694,START,119,2461,7020836
9694,BEACON,119,2461,7020836
9704,BEACON,119,2461,7020836
9714,BEACON,119,2461,7020836
9724,BEACON,119,2461,7020836
9734,BEACON,119,2461,7020836
9744,BEACON,119,2461,7020836
9754,BEACON,119,2461,7020836
9764,BEACON,119,2461,7020836
9774,BEACON,119,2461,7020836
9784,BEACON,119,2461,7020836
9794,BEACON,119,2461,7020836
9804,FINISH,119,2461,7020836
9804,START,119,2461,13767556
```

Figure 6-2. Excerpt of user listening behavior data. User 119 listened to an entire Ellington track start to finish and then started another Duke Ellington track. If beacons are every 10 seconds, how long was the first song?

Recommendations at Scale

Simulating the listening histories produces a lot of data, but it doesn't really require big data processing in order to produce billions of listening records. Analyzing the resulting logs, however, is where we have to start paying attention to what it takes to scale our system.

The Music Machine recommender system processes the user listening logs using Mahout's `ItemSimilarityJob` to build a recommendation model containing artist indicators. That computation is only part of the story. As with any realistic working system, a significant amount of plumbing code was required to convert formats between preexisting systems. Figure 6-3 shows how this was done. Note that because we used MapR, almost all the components were able to run in the cluster, including Python, Postgres, and LucidWorks.

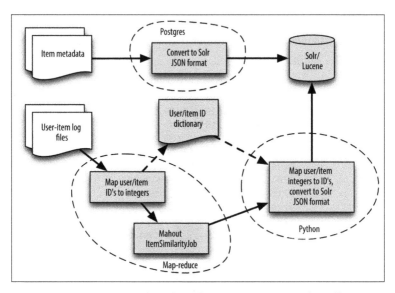

Figure 6-3. Conventional and Hadoop computing in the offline part of the recommender. Gray areas indicate parts of the Music Machine recommender that run on a Hadoop-based cluster. We used the MapR distribution for Apache Hadoop, which has a realtime distributed file system. Several extra steps would be required to use the file system found in other Hadoop distributions (HDFS).

The logs used the artist, track, and album IDs from the Postgres copy of the MusicBrainz data. These IDs are, however, not suitable directly for use with the `ItemSimilarityJob` from Mahout since that program requires that all IDs be converted to integer indexes. In our Music Machine recommender, this conversion was done using a Pig program that produced two outputs. The first output from Pig is input for the `ItemSimilarityJob`, and the second output is a dictionary that records the mapping from the original and the Mahout versions of the IDs.

Apache Mahout's `ItemSimilarityJob` processes the reindexed logs through several steps in order to look for significant co-occurrences. The output of this job contains the indicators that ultimately should go into Solr, but the artist identifiers have to be converted back from the IDs used by Mahout. This output is considerably smaller than the original user history logs, so reformatting this output and uploading the result to Solr can be done using a small Python script rather than requiring another map-reduce program in Pig. Python is easier to write and debug than Pig. For this reason, doing small steps using Python pays off in better development productivity. For data up to several hundred megabytes in size or so, Python can even be faster because it doesn't suffer the penalty of having to schedule and start an entire map-reduce program.

As is typical in big data applications, the best tool for the job depends on which job is being done. The example here uses multiple technologies, including a conventional database, map-reduce programs, higher-level languages like Pig, and conventional scripting languages like Python. Using the MapR distribution for Apache Hadoop as the basic platform simplifies the development of this recommendation system because the realtime distributed file system of MapR allows all of these components to share data transparently, without any copies or file-system conversions. Therefore, the input, the internal table files, and the output from Postgres can all live directly on the cluster. Likewise, the Pig program can read log files that were imported using the standard Linux utility rsync and can write a dictionary file that a Python script can use directly.

A secondary benefit of having all the data on a MapR cluster is that we can move processes like the Postgres database or the Python reformatting to any machine in the cluster or to edge nodes that are just outside the cluster but that have NFS access to the cluster.

This system could have been implemented on an ordinary Hadoop cluster as well, but there would have been a number of extra conversion and copy steps that would have made this example considerably more complex. Obviously, with HDFS, the non-Hadoop conventional programs would not be able to run on the cluster itself. Sharing data would require network copies.

A Peek Inside the Engine

For this project, we used Apache Solr via the commercial software product known as LucidWorks Search. LucidWorks provides considerable convenience in working with Solr by providing a comprehensive binary package with good installers and a simpler web interface than the native Solr interface provides.

Recall that data stored in Solr is organized as collections. For our music item metadata, we used one collection each for artists, albums, and tracks. In the artists collection, for example, there is a Solr document for each artist. The document contains specific information about the item in *fields* that can be indexed and made searchable by Solr's text-retrieval capabilities. In the Music Machine, this search capability is used both for textual search, such as artist by name, and for recommendations.

Figure 6-4 shows a view of the status page for the artists collection as seen using the LucidWorks administrative interface. This view is one of the different views of each collection that LucidWorks provides in its administrative interface, which gives you a convenient way to take a peek into the internals of our music recommender. Clicking on the Tools tab allows you to see additional views by searching for artist or indicator ID, or you can view the entire collection by using an empty search.

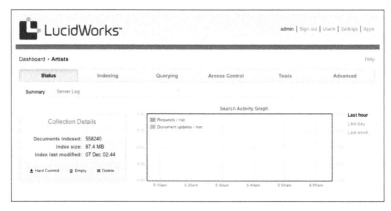

Figure 6-4. Developer view into the music recommender with the LucidWorks dashboard for the artists collection of documents. Other options include checking on which fields have been indexed or searching by artist ID, artist name, indicator IDs, or any combination of those.

The artist collection in the MusicMachine has indicator fields on only a minority of all artists. This happens because the field only appears when a value is inserted, and it is common that only a small fraction of items are statistically found to be worth recommending in the co-occurrence analysis.

Using Search to Make the Recommendations

Our demonstration program also includes a mockup of a music-listening service running using a micro web server known as Twisted Web (*http://twistedmatrix.com/trac/wiki/TwistedWeb*). This easy-to-run open source web server can be configured with Python. All the pages in the system are completely static, and all history accumulation is done using browser cookies.

To demonstrate how recommendations occur with the demo site, a user visits the Music Machine website and takes action in the form of "listening" to a song by a favorite artist—in this case, a track by classic jazz artist Duke Ellington. This behavior is retained in a browser cookie, but when a user emulates listening to a track, it also has a realtime effect: it triggers recommendations. The system does this by formatting the list of artists in the recent listening history as a query for Solr that retrieves other artists by searching for indicator artists.

Solr's search finds the best matches based on the data stored in the indicator fields of Solr documents in the artists collection. Solr computes a relevance score to determine which artists will be listed first in the recommendations.

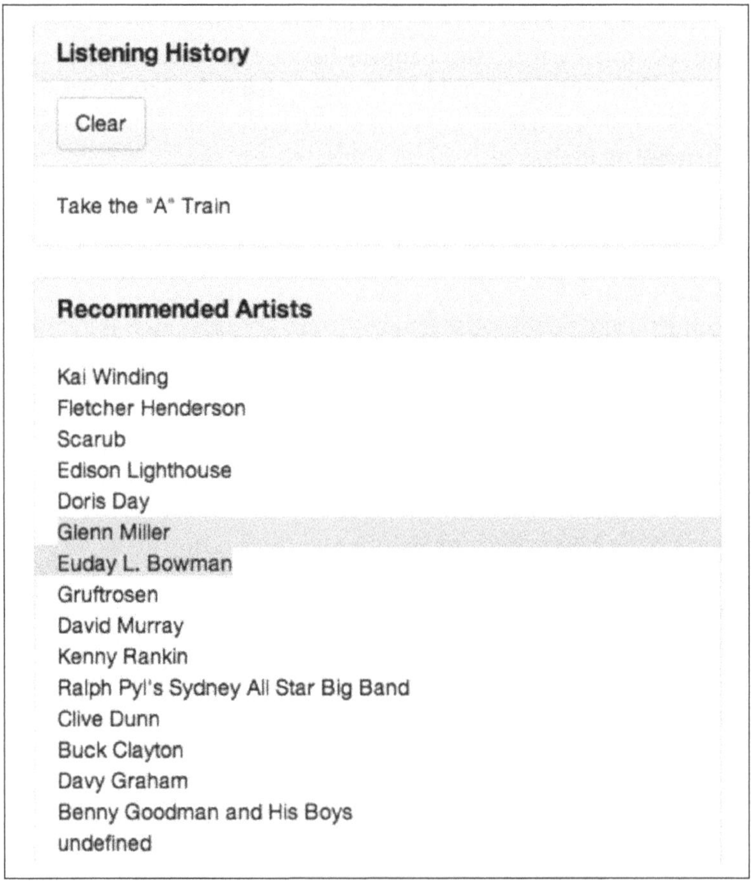

Listening History

Clear

Take the "A" Train

Recommended Artists

Kai Winding
Fletcher Henderson
Scarub
Edison Lighthouse
Doris Day
Glenn Miller
Euday L. Bowman
Gruftrosen
David Murray
Kenny Rankin
Ralph Pyl's Sydney All Star Big Band
Clive Dunn
Buck Clayton
Davy Graham
Benny Goodman and His Boys
undefined

Figure 6-5. The user's view of the Mahout–Solr/Lucene recommender in action on the Music Machine website. Recent listening history is used as a query to retrieve recommended artists for this user.

The recommendations shown in Figure 6-5 were returned to a user who listened to "Take the A Train" by Duke Ellington, as you can see in the Listening History. Notice that Benny Goodman and His Boys is also recommended but further down the list, below the highlighted artists, Glenn Miller and Euday L. Bowman—both interesting suggestions for this user.

The recommendation engine built for the Music Machine web server is a working recommender, and the results are OK, but not stellar. Why? For one thing, the user histories used to find co-occurrence and indicators were synthetic data instead of real histories for real visitors to a website. The synthetic data mimicked some aspects of the behaviors of real users, but it isn't a truly accurate representation of what people do. Another limitation is that the system was only trained on the equivalent of a few hours of data for a moderately sized website, which is not enough data to show real subtleties.

Better or larger user history is one way that a successful recommender can be made better. Chapter 7 discusses some other tips and tricks to improve your recommender.

Making It Better

The two-part design for the basic recommender we've been discussing is a full-scale system capable of producing high-quality recommendations. Like any machine-learning system, success depends in part on repeated cycles of testing, evaluation, and tuning to achieve the desired results. Evaluation is important not only to decide when a recommender is ready to be deployed, but also as an ongoing effort in production. By its nature, the model will change over time as it's exposed to new user histories—in other words, the system learns. A recommender should be evaluated not only on present performance but also on how well it is setup to perform in the future.

As we pointed out in Chapter 2, as the developer or project director, you must also decide how good is good or, more specifically, which criteria define success in your situation—there isn't just one yardstick of quality. Trade-offs are individualized, and goals must be set appropriately for the project. For example, the balance between extreme accuracy in predictions or relevance and the need for quick response or realistic levels of development effort may be quite different for a big e-commerce site when compared to a personalized medicine project. Machine learning is an automated technology, but human insight is required to determine the desired and acceptable results, and thus what constitutes success.

In practical recommendation, it's also important to put your effort where it pays off the most. In addition to the ongoing testing and adjusting to make a recommender better, there are also several add-on capabilities that are important in a real-world deployment of such a system. These add-ons are, strictly speaking, a bit outside the scope of the recommender itself and have to do with how people interact with a recommender as opposed to how a recommender works in isolation. Even if they are outside the recommender itself, these add-ons can still have a profound effect on the perceived quality of the overall recommendation system.

Dithering

The surprising thing about the technique known as *dithering* is that its approach is to make things worse in order to make them better. Recall that the order in which items are recommended depends on their relevance score. The basic approach in relevance dithering is to shake things up by intentionally including in a list of the top hits a few items with much smaller (i.e., less desirable) relevance. Why?

The idea is motivated by the observation that users don't generally look beyond the first screenful of results produced by a search or recommendation engine. You can see this if you plot the click-through rate versus result position in the search results (called rank here) for all search or recommendation results. Most likely, you will see something a lot like what's shown in Figure 7-1. Click-through will generally decline as rank increases due to decreasing relevance. At about rank 10, users will have to scroll the screen to see more results, but many won't bother. Then at rank 20, even fewer will click to the next page.

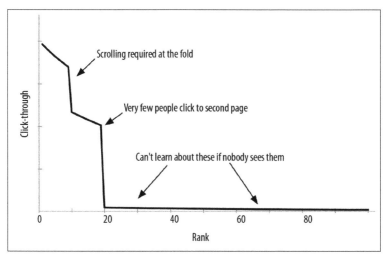

Figure 7-1. Why dithering is useful. Behavior of visitors to a website shows that recommendations that appear on the second or later pages are almost never seen by users and therefore do not provide critical feedback to the recommender.

This behavior can have a profound effect on a recommendation engine, because if users never see the results on the second and later pages, they won't provide the recommendation engine with behavioral feedback on whether these second-page results were actually any good. As a result, the recommendation engine mostly gets feedback on results that it already knows about and gets very little feedback on results at the edge of current knowledge. This limitation causes the recommendation engine to stagnate at or near the initial performance level. It does not continue to learn.

On the other hand, if the result lists are shuffled a bit, then results from the second or even later pages have a chance of appearing on the first page, possibly even above the fold. Although this change slightly dilutes the initial relevance of the top recommendations, in the long run, the system has a chance to discover excellent recommendations that it would otherwise not know about. When that happens, the engine will quickly start incorporating that discovery into mainstream results. Once again, the recommender learns.

Dithering broadens the training data that's fed to the recommendation engine. Even if accuracy is adversely impacted during the first few days of operation, the broader feedback quickly improves the accuracy well above initial levels. In fact, some recommendation-system designers have told us that introducing dithering resulted in a greater improvement in quality than any other single change.

The implementation of dithering is quite simple. One way is to take the result list and generate a score that is the log of the initial rank of each result (r) combined with normally distributed random noise. Then sort the results according to that score. This approach leaves the top few results in nearly their original order, but depending on how large the random noise is, results that would otherwise be deeply buried can be lifted onto the first page of results.

Dithering also has the surprising effect of increasing user stickiness. This happens because the recommendation page changes each time the seed for the randomization changes. It is common to keep the seed constant for minutes at a time. The change in the contents of the top few recommendations when the seed does change seems to intrigue users into repeatedly returning to the recommendation page. Paradoxically, users who don't normally click to the second page of results seem to be happy to return to the first page over and over to get additional results.

Anti-flood

Most recommendation algorithms, including the one discussed in this paper, can give you too much of a good thing. Once it zeros in on your favorite book, music, video, or whatever, any recommendation engine that works on individual items is likely to give you seemingly endless variations on the same theme if such variations can be found.

It is much better to avoid monotony in the user experience by providing diversity in recommendations with no more than a few of each kind of results. This approach also protects against having several kinds of results obscured by one popular kind. It is conceivable to build this preference for diversity into the recommendation engine itself, but our experience has been that it is much easier to ruin an otherwise good recommendation engine than it is to get diverse results out of the engine while maintaining overall quality. As a precaution, it is much easier to simply reorder the recommendations to make the results appear more diverse.

To do this, many working recommendation systems have heuristic rules known collectively as *anti-flood* measures. The way that these systems work is that they will penalize the rank of any results that appear too similar to higher-ranked results. For instance, the second song by the same artist might not be penalized, but the third song by the same artist might be penalized by 20 result positions. This example of penalizing the same artist is just one way of implementing anti-flood. Many others are plausible, and which ones work best on your data is highly idiosyncratic to your own situation.

When More Is More: Multimodal and Cross Recommendation

Throughout this discussion, we've talked about the power of simplification, but emphasized *smart* simplification. We have examined the design and functioning of a simple recommender, one in which a single kind of user interaction with a single kind of items is employed to suggest the same kind of interaction with the same kind of item. For example, we might recommend music tracks for listening based on user histories for tracks to which they and others have previously listened.

But if you have the luxury of going beyond this basic recommendation pattern, you may get much better results with a few simple additions to the design.

Here's the basis for the added design elements. People don't just do one thing (like want a pony). They buy a variety of items, listen to music, watch videos, order travel tickets, browse websites, or comment on their lives in email and social media. In all these cases, there are multiple kinds of interactions with multiple kinds of items. Data for a variety of interactions and items is often available when building a recommender, providing a way to greatly enrich the input data for your recommender model and potentially improve the quality of recommendations.

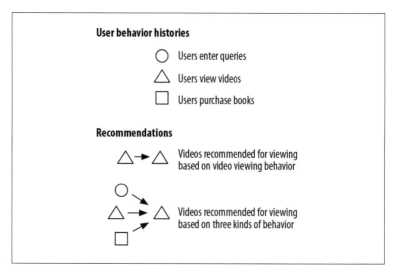

Figure 7-2. Multimodal recommendations can improve results.

The basic idea behind this multimodal approach is depicted in Figure 7-2. The first example shows a simple recommendation pattern in which there is a match between the type of interaction item and the type of recommendation. For example, you could have user-viewing histories as input data to give recommendations for video viewing, such as, "you might like to watch these videos." The triangles in Figure 7-2 illustrate this situation for the first recommendation example.

Multimodal recommendation is shown as the more complicated example in the figure. Here, more than one type of behavior is used as input data to train the recommender. Even the recent event history that triggers realtime recommendation may not be the same type of behavior as what is being recommended. In this example, for instance, book buying or a query represents a new user event. In that case, the system recommends video viewing in response to a book purchase or a query instead of in response to video viewing. Your multimodal system is using a crossover of behavior to strengthen relevance or extend the system based on which new histories are available.

As it turns out, the matrix transformations depicted back in Figure 1-2 as a "look under the covers" for a machine-learning recommender happen to represent a multimodal recommendation. While multimodal or cross-recommendations are more complicated than simple recommendations, they still are not out of reach. The good news is that the innovations already described here, such as using search technology like Solr/Lucene to deploy a recommendation system, still apply and make the next-level recommenders also relatively easy to implement.

CHAPTER 8

Lessons Learned

Real-world projects have real-world budgets for resources and effort. It's important to keep that in mind in the move from cutting-edge academic research in machine learning to practical, deployable recommendation engines that work well in production and provide profitable results. So it matters to recognize which approaches can make the biggest difference for the effort expended.

Simplifications chosen wisely often make a huge difference in the practical approach to recommendation. The behavior of a crowd can provide valuable data to predict the relevance of recommendations to individual users. Interesting co-occurrence can be computed at scale with basic algorithms such as `ItemSimilarityJob` from the Apache Mahout library, making use of log likelihood ratio anomaly-detection tests. Weighting of the computed indicators improves their ability to predict relevance for recommendations.

One cost-effective simplification is the innovative use of search capabilities, such as those of Apache Solr/Lucene, to deploy a recommender at scale in production. Search-based, item-based, recommendation underlies a two-part design for a recommendation engine that has offline learning and realtime online recommendations in response to recent user events. The result is a simple and powerful recommender that is much easier to build than many people would expect.

This two-part design for recommendation at large scale can be made easier and even more cost effective when built on a realtime distributed file system such as the one used by MapR. However, with some extra steps, this design for a recommender can be implemented on any Apache Hadoop-compatible distributed file system.

The performance quality of the recommender can generally be improved through rounds of evaluation and tuning, A/B testing, and adjustments in production, plus dithering and anti-flood tricks to keep the recommendation engine learning and keep the experience fresh for users. Furthermore, additional levels of quality can be gained by taking into account more than one type of behavior as input for the learning model: the so-called multimodal approach to recommendation.

Oh yes…and we *still* want that pony.

Additional Resources

Slides/Videos

- October 2013 Strata + Hadoop World (New York) talk by Ted Dunning on building multimodal recommendation engine using search technology: *http://slidesha.re/16juGjO*

- May 2014 Berlin Buzzwords video of "Multi-modal Recommendation Algorithms" talk by Ted Dunning: *http://bit.ly/XXy2bm*

Blog

Two related entries from Ted Dunning's blog "Surprise and Coincidence":

- On recommendation, LLR, and a bit of code: *http://bit.ly/1dCL5Vk*

- Software tutorials for corpus analysis: *http://bit.ly/1dZdKyX*

Books

- *Mahout in Action* by Sean Owen, Robin Anil, Ted Dunning, and Ellen Friedman (Manning 2011): *http://amzn.to/1eRFSbb*

  — Japanese translation: *Mahout in Action* (O'Reilly Japan): *http://bit.ly/14td9DS*

— Korean translation: *Mahout in Action* (Hanbit Media, Inc.): *http://bit.ly/VzZHY9*

- Apache Mahout Cookbook by Piero Giacomelli (Packt Publishing 2013): *http://amzn.to/1cCtQNP*

Training

One-day technical course, "Machine Learning with Apache Mahout: Introduction to Scalable ML for Developers," developed by the authors for MapR Technologies and co-developed by Tim Seears of Big Data Partnership. For details, see MapR (*http://bit.ly/1cmBl1q*) or BDP (*http://bit.ly/1mbzgor*).

Apache Mahout Open Source Project

For more information, visit the Apache Mahout website (*http://bit.ly/15lvl2x*) or Twitter (*http://twitter.com/@ApacheMahout*).

LucidWorks

The LucidWorks website (*http://bit.ly/17X2F1j*) includes tutorials on Apache Solr/LucidWorks.

Elasticsearch

Elasticsearch (*http://www.elasticsearch.org/*) provides an alternative wrapper for Lucene. The techniques in this book work just as well for Elasticsearch as for Solr.

About the Authors

Ted Dunning is Chief Applications Architect at MapR Technologies and committer and PMC member of the Apache Mahout, ZooKeeper, and Drill projects and mentor for the Apache Storm, DataFu, Flink, and Optiq projects. He contributed to Mahout clustering, classification, and matrix decomposition algorithms and helped expand the new version of Mahout Math library. Ted was the chief architect behind the MusicMatch (now Yahoo Music) and Veoh recommendation systems, built fraud-detection systems for ID Analytics (LifeLock), and is the inventor of over 24 issued patents to date. Ted has a PhD in computing science from University of Sheffield. When he's not doing data science, he plays guitar and mandolin. Ted is on Twitter at *@ted_dunning*.

Ellen Friedman is a consultant and commentator, currently writing mainly about big data topics. She is a committer for the Apache Mahout project and a contributor to the Apache Drill project. With a PhD in Biochemistry, she has years of experience as a research scientist and has written about a variety of technical topics including molecular biology, nontraditional inheritance, and oceanography. Ellen is also co-author of a book of magic-themed cartoons, *A Rabbit Under the Hat*. Ellen is on Twitter at *@Ellen_Friedman*.